GROWING HAPPY MINDS - UNLOCK POSITIVE MINDSET IN KIDS

Sushma Vaibhav

Chennai • Bangalore

CLEVER FOX PUBLISHING
Chennai, India

Published by CLEVER FOX PUBLISHING 2024
Copyright © Sushma Vaibhav 2024

All Rights Reserved.
ISBN: 978-93-56488-45-8

This book has been published with all reasonable efforts taken to make the material error-free after the consent of the author. No part of this book shall be used, reproduced in any manner whatsoever without written permission from the author, except in the case of brief quotations embodied in critical articles and reviews.

The Author of this book is solely responsible and liable for its content including but not limited to the views, representations, descriptions, statements, information, opinions and references ["Content"]. The Content of this book shall not constitute or be construed or deemed to reflect the opinion or expression of the Publisher or Editor. Neither the Publisher nor Editor endorse or approve the Content of this book or guarantee the reliability, accuracy or completeness of the Content published herein and do not make any representations or warranties of any kind, express or implied, including but not limited to the implied warranties of merchantability, fitness for a particular purpose. The Publisher and Editor shall not be liable whatsoever for any errors, omissions, whether such errors or omissions result from negligence, accident, or any other cause or claims for loss or damages of any kind, including without limitation, indirect or consequential loss or damage arising out of use, inability to use, or about the reliability, accuracy or sufficiency of the information contained in this book.

CONTENTS

About Author vii
Introduction vii
Foreword ix
Inspired Description xii

1. **Planting the Seeds: Understanding the Power of Positive Mindset** 2
   - Wh at is a positive mindset and why is it important for children?
   - The impact of negativity on childrens emotional well-being and development.
   - The connection between positive mindset and academic success, social skills and overall happiness.

2. **Cultivating Optimism: Biohacking Your Child's Happiness Toolbox** 10
   - Practical strategies for teaching children gratitude, appreciation, and reframing negative thoughts.
   - Engaging activities to build optimism and a growth mindset.
   - The power of positive self-talk and affirmations.

3. **Building Resilience: Bouncing Back Like a Boss Handling Disappointment, Frustration, and Anger** 20
   - Helping children understand and cope with emotions like disappointment, frustration, and anger.
   - Fostering problem-solving skills and a resourceful attitude.
   - The importance of celebrating effort and learning from mistakes.

4. **The Power of Connection Building Your Child's Happiness Squad** 30
   - The role of strong relationships in supporting childrens emotional well-being.
   - Fostering communication and empathy within families and communities.
   - Building positive social connections and combating bullying.

5. **Growing Happy Minds** 40
   - Creating a positive and supportive environment at home, in school, and beyond.
   - Integrating positive mindset practices into daily routines.
   - Celebrating progress and enjoying the journey.

6. **Igniting Imagination: Storytelling & Play** 50
   - The power of storytelling to shape children's beliefs and attitudes.

- Engaging storytelling activities to promote positive thinking and resilience.
- The role of play in fostering optimism and emotional well-being.

7. Taming The Inner Critic 58
- Identifying and understanding negative thought patterns.
- Strategies for reframing negative thoughts into positive ones.
- Building self-compassion and self-acceptance.

8. Celebrating Effort 66
- The dangers of perfectionism and its impact on self-esteem.
- Shifting the focus from achievement to efforts and learning.
- Celebrating small wins and encouraging perseverance.

9. Navigating the Digital World 74
- The impact of technology on childrens mental health and well-being.
- Setting healthy boundaries and responsible technology use guidelines.
- Promoting positive online engagement and digital citizenship.

10. Growing Together **82**
- Fostering a positive mindset as a family or community.
- Recognizing the importance of self-care and positive role modelling.
- Cultivating a growth mindset and embracing challenges as opportunities.

Conclusion *90*
Acknowledgements *91*

ABOUT AUTHOR

Sushma Vaibhav

This book is written by someone, who gets the challenges with Parenting. Someone who understands the real-world chaos, the tantrums, the bedtime battles and the desperate need for a sanity-saving nap (because let's be honest, raising happy humans is not a cake-walk).

I am a Software Engineer by profession, but just out of interest started following Law of Attraction videos and strategies, and Guess what it actually works. Hence thought it would help lots of parents like me to unlock Positive mindset in kids and tried crafting these well proven tricks into this Happiness Manual.

INTRODUCTION

Vision:

This book aims to empower parents, educators, and caregivers with practical tips and strategies aligned with law of attraction to help nurture positive mindset in kids. By fostering optimism, resilience, and self-belief, we can equip kids to navigate challenges with grace, bounce back from setbacks and unlock their full potential.

I'm happy to help with fostering a positive mindset in your children!

Target Audience:

This book primarily targets:

Parents: Individuals seeking to cultivate a positive and supportive environment for their children at home. It also provides some key parenting tips based on the principles of positive psychology

Educators: Teachers, counsellors, and school administrators looking to foster positive mindsets within their classrooms and school communities.

Caregivers: Relatives, babysitters, and nannies who play a significant role in shaping children's emotional development.

Additionally, the book can benefit grandparents, coaches, mentors, and other individuals who interact with and influence children's live…

Mission:

The journey to cultivate a positive mindset in children is an ongoing process. By incorporating the tools and strategies presented in this book, we can empower children to navigate life's challenges with confidence, resilience, and joy.

Broader Scope of this book is to promote law of attraction techniques over millions of people and add value in their lives by helping them to raise Successful individuals for Future Generations.

"**Unlock Positive Mindset In Kids**" invites you to embark on a transformative journey. By empowering children with the tools and strategies within these pages, we can unlock a world where optimism, resilience, and joy become the guiding principles of their lives.

FOREWORD

Crack the Code, Cultivate Joy
– Welcome to Your Kid's Happiness Hack

Hold onto your tiny humans, folks, because you're about to embark on a transformative journey. Forget the dusty parenting manuals and saccharine self-help drivel. This is no ordinary "Be H appy" book. This is an adventure guide, a mindset manual, a happiness hack for the most important people in your life: **"Our kids! Our Future Generation".**

Think of their brains as incredible biocomputers, pre-installed with the potential for joy, resilience, and grit. But just like any complex system, they need the right programming. That's where you come in, the ultimate life hacker, ready to crack the code and unlock their positive potential.

This book isn't penned by some ivory tower academic. It's written by someone who gets it. Someone who understands the real-world chaos, the tantrums, the bedtime battles, and the desperate need for a sanity-saving nap (because let's be honest, raising happy humans is not a cake walk).

But here's the good news: it doesn't have to be an uphill climb. Forget the guilt trips and the pressure to be a Perfect Parent. This isn't about moulding your kids into miniature Buddhas. It's about equipping them with the tools to navigate life's inevitable bumps with a smile (or at least a sigh that doesn't sound like the end of the world).

So, what's inside this treasure trove of kids-happiness hacks? Buckle up, because you're about to discover:

The science of joy: Dive into the fascinating neuroscience behind happiness. Understand how their brains work, and you'll unlock the secrets to fostering positive emotions.

Practical, actionable tools: No more theory, just proven strategies that you can implement starting today. From gratitude games to growth mindset mantras, you'll have a toolbox overflowing with happiness-inducing techniques.

Real-life stories: Not just dry statistics, but relatable anecdotes from parents who've been there, done that, and gotten the glitter-stained t-shirt. Learn from their triumphs and their "oops" moments, and discover what truly works (and what doesn't).

A dose of humour: Because let's face it, parenting is hilarious...in a slightly terrifying way. This book doesn't shy away from the laughter, reminding you that even amidst the meltdowns, there's always room for a giggle.

Remember, cultivating happy minds is about empowering your kids to navigate life's ups and downs with resilience, optimism, and a healthy dose of self-compassion. It's about building a foundation of emotional well-being that will serve them throughout their lives.

P.S. This book isn't a magic wand. There will be meltdowns, there will be tears, and there will be moments when you question your sanity. But with the right tools and a healthy dose of humour, you can navigate it all and raise kids who are not just happy, but equipped to thrive. Now go forth and spread the joy!

INSPIRED DESCRIPTION

Forget Gold Medals, Unlock Their Happiness: Cracking the Code to "Growing Happy Minds"

Think happiness is a participation trophy you hand out after every scraped knee? Think again. "Unlocking Positive Mindset in Kids" isn't your average "be happy" book. It's a mindset manual for the most important people in your life: your tiny happiness ninjas. We're talking neuroscience, not rainbows and kittens. Actionable tools, not fluffy platitudes. This is the journey of child development, minus the four-hour workweek (because let's be honest, parenting is a 24/7 job).

Imagine your kid's brain as a biocomputer pre-loaded with joy potential. But just like any tech, it needs the right programming. That's where you come in, the ultimate life hacker, ready to crack the code and unlock their positive superpowers.

Remember, happy kids don't just happen. They're nurtured, with the right tools and a healthy dose of self-compassion.

It's about building a foundation of emotional well-being that will serve them throughout their lives.

So, are you ready to unlock the positive potential within your precious humans? Open this book, grab your little happiness hackers, and get ready to embark on a journey that will fill your days with not just giggles, but genuine joy. Remember, happy kids lead happier lives, and guess what? That makes for pretty darn happy parents too. Now, let's get happy hacking!

LESSON 1

PLANTING THE SEEDS: UNDERSTANDING THE POWER OF POSITIVE MINDSET

Think of your kid's brain as a bio-hackable supercomputer. What you program into it today shapes how they process information, navigate challenges, and ultimately unlock their full potential. We are dealing with emotional operating systems, and the most crucial upgrade you can install is a positive mindset.

What is this "positive mindset" anyway? It's about rewiring your child's mental software to see:

Challenges as opportunities: Not roadblocks, but stepping stones to growth. Imagine Mario facing a Goomba – negativity says "game over," positivity says "bring it on!"

Setbacks as lessons: Not failures, but feedback for improvement. Think Edison's 10,000 light bulb attempts – negativity cries "quit!", positivity shouts "Yes It is Possible!"

"Can't" as a temporary glitch: This isn't a fixed-mindset prison, it's a growth-mindset playground. "I can do it" is the new "watch me!"

Why is this upgrade critical?

Because negativity is like a mental malware, draining their emotional battery and hindering their development. Imagine your child facing a math problem:

Negativity whispers: "I'm bad at math," "This is too hard," "I'll never get it."

Positivity screams: "This is a brain training puzzle," "Let's break it down step-by-step," "Mistakes are learning opportunities!"

See the difference? Negativity leads to anxiety, low self-esteem, and academic struggles. Positivity fuels resilience, confidence, and a love of learning.

The best part?

This isn't about forcing smiles or ignoring problems. It's about teaching them mental fitness hacks:

Growth mindset exercises: Help them reframe challenges as opportunities.

Gratitude practices: Shift their focus from what's lacking to what they appreciate.

Error-positive thinking: Teach them to view mistakes as learning tools.

Positive affirmations: Plant empowering beliefs like "I'm capable" and "I can learn anything."

Remember, you're their ultimate life coach. By upgrading your own positive mindset and modelling these hacks, you create a nurturing environment for your child's mental well-being to flourish. Think of it as future-proofing their happiness and success. Start planting those seeds, and watch your little superstar blossom!

This is just the first byte in our positive mindset upgrade program. Stay with me until end for more actionable hacks and science-backed strategies to empower your child's mental game and unlock their full potential!

Planting the Seeds: Dodging the Negativity Virus - How it Hurts Your Child's Development

Imagine your kid's mind as a high-performance race car. Now imagine negativity as a mental malware, slowing them down, draining their battery, and messing with their navigation system. Yup! That's the harsh reality of negativity on children's emotional well-being and development. Let's pop the hood and see what's going wrong:

- **Anxiety City:** Constant negativity breeds worry and fear, turning daily challenges into Mount Everest-sized obstacles. Picture facing a test: negativity screams "disaster!", positivity says "bring it on!"
- **Self-Esteem Crash:** Like a faulty fuel gauge, negativity tells them they're "not good enough," leading to low self-worth and a fear of trying new things. Say goodbye to exploring new hobbies, hello to hiding under the covers.
- **Social Skills Stall:** Imagine trying to make friends while wearing a "negativity force field." It's tough! Pessimism makes connecting with others challenging, hindering their social development.
- **Learning Lag:** Negativity is like a mental fog, blurring their focus and motivation. Remember struggling with homework? That's negativity at work.

This emotional malware doesn't just impact their mood, it stunts their growth across the board. Think of it as hacking their potential and leaving them lagging behind. But fear not, fellow parent-hackers! We've got the antidote:

Positive Mindset Power-Up! By installing this mental upgrade, we can:

- **Boost their emotional resilience:** Turn anxiety into excitement, fear into determination. Think of a video game character gaining power-ups!
- **Fuel their self-esteem:** Replace "not good enough" with "capable and growing." Imagine their confidence meter skyrocketing!

- **Unlock their social skills:** Trade the negativity force field for a positive aura, attracting friendships like bees to honey.
- **Ignite their learning engine:** Replace the mental fog with
- laser focus and a love for knowledge.

Remember, a positive mindset isn't about ignoring problems. It's about teaching them mental agility to navigate challenges with a "can-do" attitude. This isn't just about their happiness, it's about future-proofing their success. Let's get started on their mental upgrade and watch them zoom past negativity and unlock their full potential!

Stay with me for more actionable hacks and science-backed strategies to immunize your child against negativity and empower their emotional well-being!

Planting the Seeds: From Grump to Champ
– How Positivity Boosts Everything

Think of your kid's brain as a symphony orchestra. A positive mindset is the maestro, conducting all the sections - academics, social skills, and happiness - into a beautiful performance. But when negativity takes the lead, it's like nails on a chalkboard.

Let's break it down:

Academics: Imagine facing a math problem. Negativity whispers, "I'm bad at math," leading to frustration and giving up. Positivity shouts, "Challenge accepted!", sparking curiosity and perseverance. That "aha!" moment after figuring it out? Pure happiness fuel.

Social Skills: Picture approaching a new group. Negativity screams, "They won't like me," leading to isolation. Positivity says, "Let's make new friends!", fostering confidence and communication skills. The laughter and joy of shared experiences? Social connection gold.

Overall Happiness: Imagine a rainy day. Negativity cries, "Everything is ruined," leading to a grumpy day. Positivity says, "Time for indoor adventures!", sparking creativity and fun. The smiles, giggles, and cozy memories? Pure happiness magic.

But it's not just feel-good vibes. Research shows a positive mindset:

- **Boosts academic performance:** Students with a growth mindset learn better, persist longer, and achieve higher grades. Think straight-A superstars!
- **Improves social skills:** Positive kids build stronger friendships, communicate effectively, and handle conflicts with grace. Social butterflies, assemble!
- **Increases overall happiness:** Less stress, more resilience, and a deeper appreciation for life's little joys. Picture your child beaming like a mini-Buddha!

The key takeaway?

A positive mindset isn't just a fluffy add-on, it's a performance-enhancing drug for all areas of your child's life. Think of it as unlocking their full potential and setting them up for success and happiness, both now and in the future.

Stay with me for actionable hacks and science-backed strategies to equip your child with this ultimate success toolkit. We'll turn those frowns upside down and watch them conduct their own symphony of academic achievement, social connection, and pure, unadulterated joy!

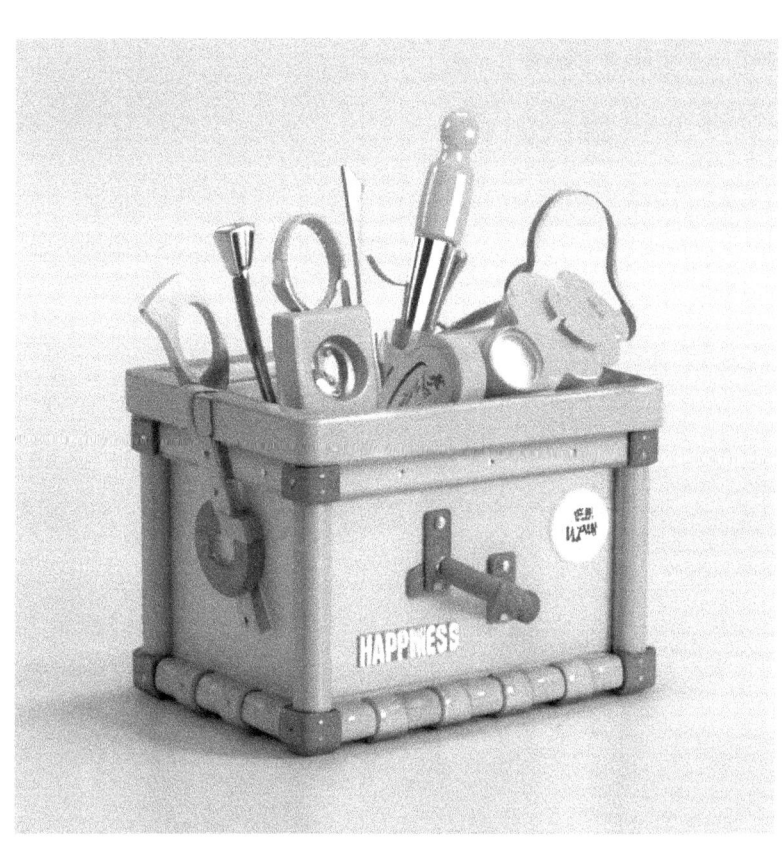

LESSON 2

CULTIVATING OPTIMISM: BIOHACKING YOUR CHILD'S HAPPINESS TOOLBOX

Remember that symphony orchestra metaphor from before? Let's add some instruments to boost your child's optimism and conduct a beautiful melody of happiness. But let go the dusty old violins and stuffy flutes – we're talking cutting-edge, science-backed tools and techniques! Buckle up, parents, it's time to bio-hack your child's brain for positivity.

Tool #1: The Gratitude Mindset:

Forget counting sheep, let's count blessings! This daily gratitude practice shifts their focus from "what they lack" to "what they have." Imagine a gratitude journal filled with "thank yous" for family, friends, even their favourite stuffed animal.

Exercise:

Make your kid write an Gratitude Journal either in book or digital or decorated chart sheets and see the magic working.

Best Practice that can be followed is Make them say thank you for any 5 things which they are grateful for. They can say Gratitude for 5 things in the morning and night. It can be simple as " Thanks for the Sun-light we get", "Thanks for Air we breathe", "Thanks for Teachers" and list is actually endless.

Can even keep an Gratitude Jar in house, and all the family members can put in the chit into the jar with their Gratitude statements. Once in a week on Sundays altogether can sit and go through those chits. Group Gratitude doubles the " Gratitude Frequency & yields Double Happiness ".

Gratitude = Happiness Amplifier.

Tool #2: The Appreciation Amplifier:

Train their appreciation muscles to see the good in everything, big or small. Think beyond "thank you for dinner" and explore the delicious flavours, the effort involved, the shared experience.

Exercise:

Encourage your kid play a game and reward them with points and gifts assign an task to them as one appreciation for someone or something every day.

Appreciation = Joy Multiplier.

Tool #3: The Reframe Renegades

Negativity alert! Don't panic, equip them with reframing superpowers. Turn "I can't do it" into "Yes I can do it", "This is hard" into "This is a challenge I can learn from," and "I messed up" into "This is a chance to grow."

Exercise:

Encourage your kid to talk Strong Positive Statements. Narrate strongly positive valued stories to them during sleep time. Encourage to watch motivational videos to make best use of their screen time.

Reframing = Inducing Positivity, Neutralising Negativity.

Tool #4: The Positive Affirmation Anthem

Words have power, especially positive ones! Craft mantras they can repeat like affirmations: "I am capable," "I am worthy," "I can learn anything."

Exercise: Paste Affirmations in their rooms, Make an Affirmation wall, Help them create an attractive diary and make them read and write Affirmations daily.

Affirmations = Confidence Booster.

Sample one is below:

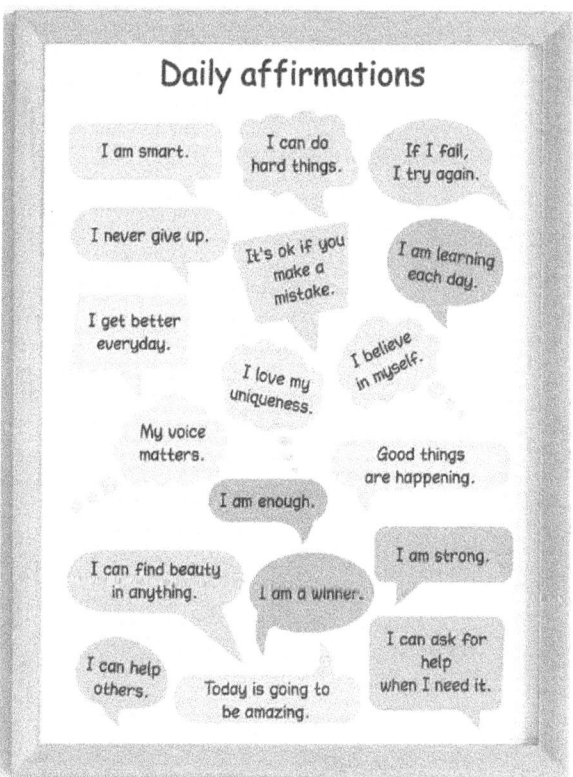

Tool #5: The Mindfulness Maestro

Teach them to quieten their minds and appreciate the present moment. Imagine deep breathing exercises, guided meditations, even mindful walks in nature.

Exercise: Identify the time of the day in which your kid feels irritated or frustrated, practice Guided Meditation, deep breathing exercises during those minutes when the negativity is at its peak.

Morning hours and during Sleep time is also best time to practice meditation because it helps them to start their day good and sleep in a Positive subconscious mode.

Mindfulness = Stress Reducer and Happiness Conductor.

Remember, these aren't just one-time tricks – it's about integrating them into their daily routine. Think of it as building a positivity fortress, brick by mindful brick, affirmation by empowering affirmation. By equipping them with these tools, you're not just giving them temporary happiness, you're setting them up for a lifetime of optimism and resilience.

Stay with me for more actionable hacks and science-backed strategies to further optimize your child's happiness toolkit.

Together, we can create a generation of optimistic champions, conducting their own symphonies of success and joy!

Cultivating Optimism:
Gamifying Growth and Happiness

Remember the symphony orchestra metaphor? Let's stop the dusty routine and inject some fun! We're talking about engaging activities that build optimism and a growth mindset like nobody's business.

Think of it as gamifying your child's happiness journey, with high scores in positivity and levels unlocked for personal growth. Buckle up, parents, it's time to transform negativity into an epic boss battle with these awesome activities!

Activity #1: The "Challenge Champion" Quest:

Forget "I can't," embrace "I can't yet!" Set weekly challenges, Celebrate progress, not just perfection, and watch their growth mindset soar.

Activity #2: The "Gratitude Galaxy" Game:

*Craft a **"Gratitude Jar"** and decorate it with stars and planets. Each day, write down something they're grateful for, adding a star to the jar. By the end of the week, they'll have a galaxy of appreciation!*

Activity #3: The "Reframe Renegades" Obstacle Course:

Set up an obstacle course (pillows, chairs, toys) and assign challenges with negative phrases ("I'm bad at this"). Help them reframe each challenge positively ("This is tough, but I can try my best!"). Completing the course becomes a celebration of overcoming negativity! Think an mental agility as the ultimate test!

Activity #4: The "Affirmation Adventure Trail":

Hide positive affirmations on a nature walk around house or park (trees, rocks, leaves). Have them find the affirmations and read them aloud, boosting their confidence and self-belief. Think treasure hunt, but with self-love as the buried gold!

Activity #5: The "Mindful Mastermind Meditation":

Guide them through simple mindfulness exercises like focusing on their breath or listening to sounds around them. Turn it into a fun competition: who can stay quiet the longest? Remember, it's not about winning, but about finding calm amidst the chaos. Inner peace as the ultimate power!

Remember, these aren't just isolated bursts of fun; weave them into the fabric of your family life. Think of it as creating a culture of optimism and growth. By making these activities engaging and playful, you're not just teaching them valuable skills, you're building a foundation for a happy, resilient future.

Stay with me till the end of the book for more actionable hacks and science-backed strategies to further optimize your child's happiness toolkit. Together, let's turn their frown upside down and watch them conquer negativity, unlock their potential, and win the ultimate prize: a life filled with optimism and joy!

Cultivating Optimism:

Programming Your Child's Inner Coach - The Power of Positive Self-Talk and Affirmations

Remember the symphony orchestra analogy? Think of your child's inner voice as the conductor. But instead of a dusty old maestro, let's install a positive self-talk powerhouse to conduct a beautiful melody of confidence and self-belief. Forget negative chatter, we're talking powerful affirmations and empowering self-talk that will have your child singing their own praises in no time!

Tool #1: The Positive Self-Talk Switch:

We all have that inner critic, but for kids, it can be especially loud. Time to flip the switch and empower them to become their own cheerleaders! Teach them to replace negative self-talk like "I'm bad at this" with positive phrases like "This is challenging, but I can learn."

Think flipping a light switch from dim to dazzling!

Switching Words creates Wonders

Tool #2: The Affirmation Arsenal:

Words have power, especially positive ones! Craft powerful affirmations they can repeat like mantras: "I am capable," "I am worthy," "I can believe in myself."

Think affirmations as mental armour, deflecting negativlty and boosting confidence!

Create Affirmation Boards and paste them around the house

Tool #3: The Visualization Technique:

Help them visualize success. Ask them to imagine themselves conquering their fears, achieving their goals, and feeling proud. This "mental rehearsal" builds confidence and motivation.

Think training for a sports competition, but visualizing victory in the mind's eye!

Create Visualization Boards with an photo of your Kid and Goal achieved, Paste them around the house.

Tool #4: The "Mirror, Mirror" Magic:

Stand in front of the mirror together and repeat positive affirmations aloud. Seeing themselves say these empowering words creates a powerful connection between mind and body.

Tool #5: The "Role Model Remix":

Show your child examples of positive self-talk from inspiring figures in their life or stories. Discuss how these individuals overcame challenges with self-belief.

Think learning from superheroes, but with real-life role models as the inspiration!

Think of creating an Mentor Wall at your Kid's room by placing the photographs of their Mentors and Role Models, club them with kid's photo so that they imbibe the qualities looking at the picture together.

Remember, this isn't a one-time fix; it's about integrating these tools into their daily routine. Think of it as building a fortress of positivity, brick by empowering affirmation, brick by positive self-talk. By equipping them with these tools, you're not just giving them temporary confidence, you're setting them up for a lifetime of self-belief and resilience.

Stay tuned till the end for more actionable hacks and science-backed strategies to further optimize your child's happiness toolkit. Together, let's silence their inner critic, amplify their positive voice, and watch them conduct their own symphony of self-love and success!

LESSON 3

BUILDING RESILIENCE: BOUNCING BACK LIKE A BOSS HANDLING DISAPPOINTMENT, FRUSTRATION, AND ANGER

Remember the **symphony orchestra** analogy? Imagine life throws a curveball – a missed goal, a lost toy, a friend's disagreement. The negativity monster whispers, "Game over!" But we're not raising whiners, we're training **resilient champions!** Let's equip them with **ninja-level emotional agility** to **bounce back from challenges and conduct their own victory tune.** Buckle up, parents, it's time to **bio-hack their coping mechanisms and turn setbacks into stepping stones!**

Tool #1: The Emotion Expedition:

Help them **identify and understand their emotions.** Disappointment stings, frustration simmers, anger roars. Teach them to name it, not shame it. Think emotional intelligence training, but with "Inside Out" characters as guides!

Be a friend of your kid and instead of judging them or declaring conclusions, sit along and discuss what they are feeling and let the emotions flow, so that you can gauge where your kid stands emotionally and help to re-program.

Tool #2: The "Calm Down Corner" Refuge:

Create a designated space for them to **regulate their emotions healthily.** Deep breathing exercises, calming music, mindfulness activities – it's their personal stress-busting haven. Think of it as a mental spa, but without the cucumber slices!

Can place and photo of their favourite God/Goddess or rock or anything that best suites your kid, place it at some corner of the house, declare it as Me Corner for your kid where he/she can have some Me-time and realise true feelings, so that they don't fill in negativity deep inside. Few unsaid words, unexpressed feelings come out over here and lightens oneself."Self Love" should be practiced over "Me Corner".

Tool #3: The "Reframe Remix":

Challenges aren't roadblocks, they're **learning opportunities.** Help them reframe disappointment as "This didn't work, but I can try again differently," frustration as "This is tough, but I can figure it out," and anger as "I'm feeling upset, but I can express it calmly."

Think growth mindset on steroids, turning setbacks into fuel for progress!

Talk to your kids, make them feel it's Not a Big Deal to Fail, but can re-work and succeed over failures. Reframe the Thought Process, teach them to stand-up, rise after the fall.

Tool #4: The "Problem-Solving Power Up":

Don't just fix their problems, **coach them to solve them themselves.** Guide them through brainstorming solutions, evaluating options, and taking action.

Try to put up small challenging activities depending on your kids age & capability, watch them overcome, guide and appreciate their Problem-Solving capacities. So that they gain confidence on Self Ability.

Tool #5: The "Celebrate Small Victories" Party:

Resilience isn't about avoiding challenges, it's about **celebrating progress.** Acknowledge their efforts, no matter how small. A high five for trying a new game, a cheer for calming down, a fist bump for expressing their feelings – small wins build big resilience!

Think victory dances after each step, not just reaching the finish line!

A hug & kiss, A Pat on their Back, Small appreciations, Gifts shared over their victories works magic in Kids Mental WellBeing.

Say No to Comparison, Please do not compare your kids with others instead of congratulating them on their victories.

Remember, resilience isn't built overnight. It's a **muscle that needs constant training.** By equipping them with these tools, you're not just teaching them coping mechanisms, you're **building an emotional fortress** that will weather any storm life throws their way. They'll learn to **bounce back stronger, wiser, and ready to conduct their own symphony of success!**

Stay tuned for more **actionable hacks and science-backed strategies** to further **optimize your child's emotional resilience toolkit.** Together, let's empower them to face any challenge, **turn setbacks into stepping stones, and ultimately conduct their own beautiful melody of resilience and happiness!**

Building Resilience: From Grump to Champ Problem-Solving Power-Ups and Resourceful Remakes

Remember the **symphony orchestra** analogy? Imagine life throws a curveball – a broken toy, a forgotten homework assignment, a fight with a friend. The negativity gremlins whisper, "Disaster!" But we're not raising drama queens, we're training **resilient champions!** Let's equip them with **ninja-level problem-solving skills and a resourceful attitude** to **turn setbacks into springboards and conduct their own victory tunes.** Buckle up, parents, it's time to **bio-hack their resourcefulness and transform challenges into epic quests**

Tool #1: The Brainstorming Bonanza:

Forget meltdowns, embrace **brainstorming sessions!** When faced with a challenge, guide them through creative problem-solving. Th ink outside the box, list wild ideas, encourage laughter – it's all about generating possibilities.

Think brainstorming like a superhero team planning to defeat a villain, but with everyday challenges as the enemies!

Tool #2: The "Best Use of Resources Available" Challenge:

Channel the spirit of the resourceful hero! Encourage them to find creative solutions using what they have. Cardboard fort becomes spaceship? Check! Old clothes become superhero costume? Absolutely! **Think resourcefulness like surviving in the wilderness, but with household items as the tools!**

Tool #3: The "Trial and Error Tango":

Mistakes happen, but they're **stepping stones, not stumbling blocks.** Teach them to embrace trial and error as part of the learning process. Celebrate each attempt, analyse what didn't work, and adjust their approach. **Think Edison's light bulb experiment, but with everyday challenges as the inventions!**

Tool #4: The "Help Me!" Lifeline:

We all need help sometimes. Teach them to **ask for help appropriately** from parents, teachers, or friends. Collaboration is key! Think of it as seeking guidance from a wise mentor..

Tool #5: The "Victory Dance" Celebration:

Problem solved, challenge conquered! Time to **celebrate their resourcefulness and resilience.** High fives, fist bumps, silly dances – anything goes! Positive reinforcement fuels future problem-solving prowess.

Think victory celebrations after winning a video game, but with real-life challenges as the conquered foes!

Remember, **resilience isn't just about bouncing back, it's about bouncing forward, stronger and more resourceful.** By equipping them with these tools, you're not just teaching them problem-solving skills, you're **building a mental toolbox** that will empower them to tackle any obstacle life throws their way. They'll learn to **think creatively, adapt on the fly, and celebrate their resourcefulness, conducting their own beautiful melody of resilience and success!**

Stay tuned till the end for more **actionable hacks and science-backed strategies** to further **optimize your child's resilience toolkit.** Together, let's empower them to **face any challenge with a resourceful spirit, turn setbacks into springboards, and ultimately conduct their own beautiful symphony of resilience and happiness!**

Building Resilience: From Grump to Champ - Celebrating Effort & Earning From Flubs

Remember our symphony orchestra metaphor? Imagine the inevitable curveball life throws: a missed goal, a forgotten homework, a squabble with a friend. The negativity gremlins hiss, "Disaster!" But we're not raising drama queens and kings, we're training resilient champions! Let's equip them with ninja-level resilience by celebrating effort and learning from mistakes, transforming setbacks into springboards and conducting their own victory tunes.

Buckle up, parents, it's time to biohack their growth mindset and turn challenges into epic quests!

Tool #1: The Effort Emporium:

Forget gold stars and participation trophies, embrace effort appreciation! When faced with a challenge, acknowledge their hard work, not just the outcome. Did they give it their all? Did they learn something new? Think of celebrating the training a wrestler, but instead of muscles, focus on the effort and sweat!

Tool #2: The "Mistakes Make Masters" Museum:

Mistakes are inevitable, but they're stepping stones, not roadblocks. Teach them to view them as learning opportunities, not failures. Every wrong answer is a chance to learn the right one, every spill is a chance to get better control. Think of Edison's light bulb experiment, but instead of the final invention, celebrate each failed attempt that led to the discovery!

Tool #3: The "Growth Mindset Groove":

It's not about never making mistakes, it's about learning from them. Guide them through analysing what went wrong, why it went wrong, and how to do it better next time. It's not about erasing yesterday's mistakes, it's about using them to fuel tomorrow's success! Think of video game characters learning from their mistakes and leveling up, but with real-life challenges as the obstacles!

Tool #4: The "High Five for Honesty" Habit:

Transparency is key to resilience. Teach them to honestly admit their mistakes when seeking help. It builds trust, opens up communication channels, and paves the way for a collaborative solution. Think of calling for help in a video game, but instead of a virtual teammate, it's a real-life parent or teacher!

Tool #5: The "Resilience Remix":

Challenges tackled, lessons learned, time to celebrate! High fives, fist bumps, silly dances - anything goes! Positive reinforcement fuels future resilience and a growth mindset. Think of Mario collecting coins after overcoming a challenge in a video game, but with real-life challenges as the conquered levels!

Remember, resilience isn't just about bouncing back, it's about bouncing forward, stronger and wiser. By equipping them with these tools, you're not just teaching them to cope with mistakes, you're building a mental muscle that will empower them to learn from every experience, grow from every challenge, and ultimately, conduct their own beautiful symphony of resilience and success!

Stay tuned for more actionable hacks and science-backed strategies to further optimize your child's resilience toolkit. Together, let's empower them to face any challenge with a growth mindset, transform setbacks into springboards, and ultimately conduct their own beautiful symphony of resilience and happiness!

LESSON 4

THE POWER OF CONNECTION BUILDING YOUR CHILD'S HAPPINESS SQUAD

Remember the symphony orchestra metaphor? Imagine your child as the conductor, but instead of instruments, they're leading a powerful ensemble of positive relationships. These connections are the emotional fuel that drives their well-being, resilience, and overall happiness. Think of it as biohacking their social life for joy and success! Buckle up, parents, it's time to orchestrate a vibrant social circle and watch your child conduct their own symphony of connection!

The Why:

Forget social media likes, focus on real-life connections. Strong relationships act as emotional shock absorbers, buffering stress, boosting confidence, and providing a safe space to express themselves. Imagine a friend as a superhero sidekick, always there to lend a hand (or a listening ear).

The Tools:

- **The "Squad Goals" Mission:**

Help them build a diverse group of positive friends who share their interests and values. Think quality over quantity: a few genuine connections are more powerful than a crowd of acquaintances.

- **The "Communication Craft":**

Teach them the art of communication: active listening, empathy, and expressing their feelings clearly. Think of it as mastering a musical instrument to create beautiful harmonies with others.

- **The "Conflict Conductor":**

Guide them through navigating disagreements healthily. Teach them to see conflict as an opportunity to learn and grow, not a reason to shut down. Think of resolving conflict like conducting a complex piece, requiring patience, understanding, and collaboration.

- **The "Family First" Foundation:**

Remember, you're their ultimate support system. Build a strong, loving family bond where they feel safe, heard, and appreciated. Think of your family as the orchestra's core ensemble, providing the bedrock of love and support.

- **The "Community Chorus":**

Expand their social circle beyond their immediate friend group. Encourage them to join clubs, sports teams, or volunteer activities. Think of it as adding new sections to the orchestra, enriching their social tapestry with diverse experiences.

The Impact:

Strong relationships aren't just feel-good vibes; they have a tangible impact on your child's development.

Studies show they:

- **Boost academic performance:** Feeling supported and connected reduces stress and fuels motivation to learn. Imagine a student playing their part in the orchestra with confidence, knowing their teammates have their back.

- **Improve social skills:** Strong relationships are the training ground for communication, empathy, and conflict resolution. Picture them navigating social situations with grace, like a maestro conducting a harmonious performance.

- **Enhance mental well-being:** Feeling connected reduces loneliness, anxiety, and depression. Think of a symphony orchestra playing in perfect harmony, creating a beautiful soundscape of happiness and well-being.

Remember, building strong relationships takes time, effort, and intentionality. By equipping them with these tools and fostering a supportive environment, you're not just giving them temporary social connections, you're setting them up for a lifetime of happiness, resilience, and the ability to conduct their own beautiful symphony of life!

Stay tuned for more actionable hacks and science-backed strategies to further optimize your child's social connection toolkit. Together, let's help them build a strong and supportive network, transform isolation into connection, and ultimately conduct their own beautiful melody of social success and happiness!

The Power of Connection
Building Your Child's Empathy Network

Remember the symphony orchestra metaphor? Imagine your child as the conductor, but forget fancy melodies – this time, their music is all about connection and empathy. These chords aren't just harmony for the ears, they're the emotional backbone of your child's well-being, resilience, and happiness. Think of it as biohacking their social life for success and joy! Buckle up, parents and communities, it's time to orchestrate a vibrant network of empathy and watch your children conduct their own symphony of connection!

The Why:

Forget social media likes, focus on real-life understanding. Strong connections with family, friends, and community act as emotional shock absorbers, buffering stress, boosting confidence, and providing safe spaces to express themselves. Imagine a friend, family member, or neighbour as a superhero sidekick, always there to lend a hand (or a listening ear) with empathy and understanding.

The Tools:

- **The "Empathy Experiment":**

Help children step into other people's shoes through storytelling, role-playing, and open discussions about feelings. Think of it as trying on different instruments in the orchestra, understanding how each part contributes to the whole.

- **The "Effective Communication":**

Teach the art of active listening, respectful communication, and expressing feelings clearly.

- **The "Family First (Mom & Dad – Are Friends)" Foundation:**

Remember, you're the ultimate empathy role model. Build a strong, loving friendly bond where open communication and understanding are the norm. Think of your family as the group of best friends who ensemble, demonstrating empathy daily through interactions.

- **The "Community Chorus":**

Expand their empathy circle beyond their immediate friend group. Encourage them to interact with diverse individuals and communities, understanding different perspectives and experiences. Think of it as adding new sections to the orchestra, enriching their empathy tapestry with the richness of human experience.

The Impact:

Empathy isn't just a feel-good buzzword; it's a life skill with powerful benefits:

- **Reduced Conflict:**
Understanding others reduces misunderstandings and fosters conflict resolution skills. Imagine the orchestra playing in perfect harmony, not because they're identical, but because they respect and appreciate each other's differences.

- **Increased Social Awareness:** Empathy promotes inclusivity and acceptance, reducing bullying and fostering a sense of belonging. Think of a vibrant community orchestra where every instrument, regardless of its sound, is valued for its unique contribution.

- **Enhanced Mental Well-Being:** Feeling connected and understood reduces loneliness, anxiety, and depression. Picture a beautiful soundscape created by the orchestra, not just for the audience, but for the joy and connection experienced by the musicians themselves.

Remember, building empathy takes intentionality and practice. By equipping children with these tools and fostering a culture of communication and understanding within families and communities, you're not just giving them temporary social skills, you're setting them up for a lifetime of happiness, resilience, and the ability to conduct their own beautiful symphony of life, where every note resonates with empathy and connection!

Stay tuned for more actionable hacks and science-backed strategies to further optimize your child's empathy toolkit. Together, let's build a symphony of understanding and connection, transforming isolation into belonging, and ultimately conducting our own beautiful melody of social success and happiness!

The Power of Connection
Building Your Child's Anti-Bullying Brigade

Remember the symphony orchestra metaphor? Imagine your child as the conductor, but this time, they're raising the baton against a harsh reality: bullying. But fear not, parents and communities! We're not raising victims, we're building an anti-bullying brigade through the power of positive social connections. Think of it as biohacking their social life for resilience and empowerment! Buckle up, it's time to orchestrate a vibrant network of support and watch your child conduct their own anti-bullying symphony!

The Why:

Forget isolating silence, focus on building a fortress of connection. Strong social bonds act as shields against bullying, boosting confidence, providing safe spaces to confide, and empowering bystanders to intervene. Imagine a friend as a superhero sidekick, always there to stand up for what's right.

The Tools:

- **The "Squad Goals" Mission:** Help them build a diverse group of positive friends who share their values and support each other. Think quality over quantity: a few genuine connections are more powerful than a crowd of acquaintances.

- **The "Communication Craft":** Teach them the art of assertive communication, setting boundaries, and reporting incidents confidently. Think of it as mastering a musical instrument to create a powerful voice against negativity.

- **The "Bystander Boost":** Empower them to be upstanders, not bystanders. Teach them to intervene safely and report bullying they witness. Think of it as conducting the entire orchestra to play a unified melody of support and intervention.

- **The "Community Chorus":** Expand their social circle beyond their immediate friend group. Encourage them to join clubs, sports teams, or volunteer activities, fostering a sense of belonging and community support. Think of it as adding new sections to the orchestra, enriching their social tapestry with diverse allies.

The Impact:

Positive connections aren't just feel-good vibes; they're weapons against bullying:

- **Reduced risk of victimization:** Feeling supported and having a strong social network decreases the likelihood of being targeted. Imagine a well-rehearsed orchestra, each instrument confident and protected by the collective harmony.

- **Increased resilience:** Positive connections provide emotional support and coping mechanisms to deal with bullying experiences. Picture them navigating challenges with strength, knowing they have their "orchestra" behind them.

- **Empowered bystanders:** A strong community encourages intervention and discourages bullying behaviour. Think of the entire orchestra playing a powerful piece against negativity, creating a culture of respect and support.

Remember, building resilience and combating bullying takes collective action. By equipping children with these tools and fostering a culture of positive connections within families, schools, and communities, you're not just giving them temporary support, you're creating a world where every child can conduct their own symphony of safety, acceptance, and belonging, silencing the discord of bullying once and for all!

Stay tuned for more actionable hacks and science-backed strategies to further optimize your child's anti-bullying toolkit. Together, let's build a symphony of unity and empower our children to conduct their own beautiful melody of a world free from bullying!

LESSON 5

GROWING HAPPY MINDS

Conducting the Symphony of Wellbeing

Remember the **symphony orchestra** metaphor? We've explored each instrument – positive mindset, resilience, communication, empathy, and connection. Now, it's time to **assemble them into a harmonious masterpiece – your child's happy mind!** Think of it as **conducting their personal orchestra of wellbeing, playing a beautiful melody that resonates throughout their lives.**

Buckle up, parents, teachers, and community leaders, it's time to **orchestrate a supportive environment where every child thrives!**

The Stage:

Forget isolated interventions, focus on **holistic well-being.** Create a **symphony of support** across home, school, and community, each playing its part in harmonizing your child's development. Think of it as building a concert hall with acoustics so perfect, every note of potential can flourish.

The Conductor:

Remember, you're the **lead conductor** in your child's life. Model optimism, communication, and empathy. Foster open communication and provide a safe space to express emotions. Think of yourself as the maestro, setting the tone and guiding the orchestra with love and understanding.

The Home Harmony:

- **Nurture positive rituals:** Family dinners, game nights, bedtime stories – create routines that foster connection and joy.

- **Encourage gratitude:** Practice daily gratitude exercises, appreciating the little things that make life beautiful.

- **Celebrate effort:** Recognize their hard work, not just the outcome, building a growth mindset.

- **Open communication:** Create a safe space for open and honest conversations about everything.

- **Model empathy:** Show compassion and understanding, teaching them to do the same.

The School Symphony:

- **Positive school climate:** Advocate for a school environment that fosters respect, inclusion, and emotional well-being.

- **Social-emotional learning (SEL):** Integrate SEL programs that teach communication, empathy, and conflict resolution.

- **Anti-bullying initiatives:** Implement strong anti-bullying policies and empower students to be upstanders.

- **Celebrate diversity:** Embrace cultural differences and create a sense of belonging for all students.

- **Open communication:** Foster collaboration between parents, teachers, and students to address challenges and celebrate successes.

The Community Chorus:

- **Positive extracurricular activities:** Encourage participation in sports, clubs, or volunteer work that builds social connections and develops talents.

- **Mentorship programs:** Connect children with caring adults who can offer guidance and support.

- **Community events:** Participate in events that promote inclusion, diversity, and positive social interaction.

- **Combat negative influences:** Address issues like cyberbullying and negative media representations head-on.

- **Advocate for change:** Work together to create a community that prioritizes child well-being and social-emotional development.

Remember, fostering happy minds is a continuous performance, not a one-time act. By working together across homes, schools, and communities, we can create a world where every child has the opportunity to ***conduct their own symphony of happiness, resilience, and success.*** The music they play will echo through their lives, creating a beautiful melody for themselves and everyone around them.

Stay tuned for more ***actionable hacks and science-backed strategies*** to further ***optimize your child's well-being toolkit.*** Together, let's raise a generation of ***confident, compassionate, and thriving individuals, conducting their own beautiful symphonies of life!***

Growing Happy Minds
Daily Rituals for a Thriving Symphony

Remember the symphony orchestra metaphor? We've explored each instrument – positive self-talk, resilience, communication, empathy, and connection – but now it's time to conduct them into a harmonious masterpiece: your child's happy mind! Think of it as orchestrating a daily symphony of well-being, woven into the fabric of their routine. Buckle up, parents, it's time to bio-hack their happiness with powerful practices!

Forget magic tricks, focus on mindful moments. We're not aiming for one-time fixes, but for integrating positive practices into their daily rhythm. Think of it as tuning each instrument individually before the grand performance.

The Mindset Maestro:

- **Morning Magic:** Start the day with a positive affirmation ritual. Help them craft empowering statements like "Yes, It is Possible", "I am capable," "I am worthy," and repeat them like mantras to set the tone for the day.

- **Gratitude Groove:** Before bedtime, take a few minutes for gratitude journaling. Reflect on three things they're grateful for, shifting their focus to the good in their lives.

- **Visualization Vault:** Encourage them to visualize success before tackling challenges. Imagine them picturing themselves conquering their goals, fuelling their confidence and motivation. Best time would be the magic minutes when kid is about to enter Good Night Sleep mode.

The Resilience Rockstar:

- **"Deep Breaths, No Freaks" Breaks:** Teach them calming breathing (Breathe-In, Breathe-Out) exercises for moments of frustration or anger. Think of it as a quick reset button, re-centering their emotions before reacting impulsively.

- **"Challenge Accepted" Attitude:** When faced with difficulties, guide them to reframe them as learning opportunities. Instead of "I can't do this," encourage them to say, "This is tough, but I can learn from it", "Yes, It is Possible", "I am a Champion" etc.

- **"Problem-Solving Power Up":** Equip them with a problem-solving toolkit. Brainstorm solutions together, analyse what went wrong, and encourage them to try again with a new approach.

The Connection Chorus:

- **"Family Feasts, Not Fast Food"**: Make mealtimes opportunities for connection. Put away screens, engage in conversation, and create positive memories together.

- **"Express Yourself Extravaganza"**: Encourage open communication by actively listening to their feelings and thoughts. Create a safe space where they can express themselves freely – Always be a best friend to your kids so that they feel safe to share even their weaknesses, mistakes, so that I feel comfortable and be sure that they are not gonna be judged by you or will be loved and accepted in any scenario. Make them confident that you will guide them in correct way & accompany them in every step.

- **"Squad Goals" Missions:** Foster strong friendships by helping them build a circle of positive, supportive peers. Encourage quality time spent together, building healthy social connections.

Remember, consistency is key. By embedding these practices into their daily routine, you're not just giving them temporary tools, you're building a foundation for lifelong happiness and resilience. Their symphony of well-being will grow stronger with each mindful moment, conducted by the maestro within – your child's empowered and optimistic self.

Stay tuned for more actionable hacks and science-backed strategies to further optimize your child's happiness toolkit. Together, let's raise a generation of confident, compassionate, and thriving individuals, each conducting their own beautiful symphony of life..

Growing Happy Minds
Applause Breaks & Encore Performances

Remember the symphony orchestra metaphor? We've assembled the instruments – positive mindset, resilience, communication, empathy, and connection – and conducted them into a beautiful melody of well-being. But wait, this isn't just a one-time concert! It's a lifelong performance, filled with applause breaks and encore opportunities. Buckle up, parents, teachers, and community champions, it's time to celebrate progress and turn the journey into its own reward!

Ditch the finish line mentality, focus on the joyful steps. We're not chasing some distant achievement, we're savouring the process of growth and celebrating every milestone. Think of it as appreciating each individual musician's contribution, not just the final grand finale.

The Celebration Conductor:

- **Appreciative Eyes:** Instead of fixating on flaws, acknowledge their effort and progress. Point out improvements, no matter how small, and shower them with genuine praise.

- **Failure Fiesta:** Reframe mistakes as opportunities to learn and grow. Throw a "learning party" after challenges, celebrating the lessons learned, not the missteps.

- **Gratitude Galaxy:** Celebrate even the little things. Encourage them to express gratitude for everyday joys, big and small, building a positive outlook.

The Journey Joyride:

- **Make mindfulness moments magical:** Transform difficult tasks into mindful adventures. Turn brushing teeth into a "sparkle smile mission" or walking to school into a "nature treasure hunt."

- **Connect with nature:** Spend time outdoors, appreciating the beauty and wonder of the natural world. Hike, garden, or simply sit under a tree, fostering a sense of peace and connection.

- **Embrace silly time:** Laughter is the best medicine! Have dance parties, tell jokes, and create playful memories together. Injecting joy into daily life fuels resilience and well-being.

Remember, happiness isn't a destination, it's a journey. By celebrating progress, enjoying the present moment, and infusing joy into everyday experiences, you're not just giving them temporary happiness, you're teaching them to savour the symphony of life itself. Their performance will evolve, grow, and change, always conducted by the maestro within – their own inner spark of joy and resilience.

Stay tuned for more actionable hacks and science-backed strategies to further optimize your child's happiness toolkit. Together, let's raise a generation of individuals who not only achieve, but also thrive, celebrating every note of their beautiful, joyful journey!

BONUS PAGE

Rituals That Teach Responsibility

- Assign each family member a specific task when setting the table
- Create a rotating chore chart on a whiteboard that changes each Sunday.
- Choose a particular time each week when the entire family comes together to clean the house.
- Find projects that the entire family can collaborate on (shelling peas, painting a wall, etc.)

Rituals That Promote Kindness & Compassion

- Practice Loving Kindness Meditation: think of your loved ones and send them positive thoughts. Say, "May you feel safe. May you feel happy. May you feel healthy."
- Find a place to volunteer as a family (a nursing home, an animal shelter, etc.)
- Have each family member share one kind thing they did that day.

Rituals That Boost Positivity

- "Family cuddle time" - when everyone arrives home, pile into bed together and cuddle for five minutes.
- Play "High, Low, Buffalo" - each family member shares the high and the low points of their day, then anything else they would like to share ("Buffalo")

Rituals That Build Strong Family Connection

- End each evening with a calming massage before bed.
- Choose a few favorite songs to use as "goodnight songs."
- Choose a few favorite stories that you read each night.
- Say, "Goodnight, nose!" while tweaking your child's nose, then, "Goodnight, toes!", and so on.
- Before saying good-night, say, "Mommy loves you. Daddy loves you. Grandma loves you," and so on.
- Have each family member contribute something to dinner preparation.
- Take turns cooking everyone's favorite meals.
- Sample dinners from different cultures each month.
- Have weekly "theme" dinners, like Taco Tuesday, Pizza Fridays, etc.

Rituals That Develop a Sense of Belonging

- Create special greetings and farewells like "See you later, alligator!"
- Have a personalized handshake with each of your children.
- Go on a hayride each year around the holidays.
- During the holidays sing songs that hold significance to your family.
- On New Year's Eve, watch family videos to reflect on the year.
- Keep a "Gratitude Jar" throughout the year.
- Make a special cake for each family member's birthday.
- On birthdays, allow kids to eat anything they want for breakfast!
- Invent and celebrate family holidays like Kid's Day
- Go on monthly (or weekly) nature walks.
- Create a theme night like a board game night or a movie night
- Have pancakes each Sunday morning.
- Camp out in the living room monthly or every so often.

BIG LIFE JOURNAL - BIGLIFEJOURNAL.COM

LESSON 6

IGNITING IMAGINATION: STORYTELLING & PLAY

Biohacking Happiness with Make-Believe

Remember the symphony orchestra metaphor? We've fine-tuned the instruments – positive mindset, resilience, communication, empathy, and connection – but now it's time to infuse their symphony with the magic of imagination! Storytelling and play aren't just fun and games; they're powerful tools for biohacking happiness and shaping positive beliefs. Buckle up, parents, teachers, and creativity champions, it's time to conduct an imaginative adventure, where every child becomes the hero of their own story!

Forget passive entertainment, focus on active engagement. We're not talking about mindless screen time, but about the interactive power of storytelling and play. Think of it as composing a melody together, where children actively participate in shaping the narrative and exploring possibilities.

The Storytelling Sage:

- **Bedtime Bonanzas:**

Craft positive, empowering bedtime stories. Focus on themes of courage, kindness, and overcoming challenges. Remember, heroes come in all shapes and sizes – let their imagination soar!

- **Interactive Adventures:**

Transform everyday moments into interactive stories. Turn grocery shopping into a treasure hunt, or a walk in the park into a quest for mythical creatures.

- **Mirror, Mirror on the Wall:**

Encourage them to act out stories, express emotions through characters, and explore different perspectives. Think of it as giving them a stage to rehearse their own unique symphony of life.

The Playful Powerhouse:

- **Open-Ended Playdays:**

Keep aside structured activities and embrace open-ended play. Provide simple materials like blocks, dress-up clothes, or art supplies, and let their imagination take the lead.

- **Cooperative Creations:**

Encourage collaborative play with friends or siblings. Building forts, writing stories together, or putting on plays fosters communication, empathy, and problem-solving skills.

- **Nature's Playground:**

Spend time outdoors, exploring, creating, and connecting with nature. The natural world ignites curiosity, encourages movement, and reduces stress, contributing to overall well-being.

- **Colouring their Imagination:**

Again it depends on their interests, but drawing and colouring, origami or other crafts used to represent their imaginations can lead to mind openness.

Remember, imagination is a muscle that needs exercise. By weaving storytelling and play into their daily lives, you're not just giving them temporary entertainment, you're equipping them with the power to shape their own narratives, build positive beliefs, and conduct their own beautiful symphony of imagination and resilience.

Stay tuned for more actionable hacks and science-backed strategies to further optimize your child's imagination toolkit. Together, let's raise a generation of creative thinkers, problem-solvers, and dreamers, ready to write their own happy endings!

Igniting Imagination: Playful Hacks for Happiness & Optimism

Biohacking Optimism with Make-Believe Adventures

Remember the grand symphony orchestra metaphor? We've tuned the instruments – positive mindset, resilience, communication, empathy, and connection – but now it's time to ignite their symphony with the magic of imagination! Forget passive entertainment, we're talking about engaging storytelling activities that biohack happiness and cultivate optimistic thinking like nobody's business. Buckle up, parents, teachers, and creativity champions, it's time to conduct an imaginative adventure, where every child transforms into the hero of their own epic tale!

Ditch the script, embrace interactive magic. We're not talking about one-way lectures here, but about the interactive power of storytelling and play. Think of it as collaboratively composing a masterpiece, where children actively participate in shaping the narrative and exploring endless possibilities.

The Storytelling Superhero:

- **Bedtime Brainstorms:**

Instead of pre-written stories, turn bedtime into a collaborative brainstorming session. Start with a simple prompt ("Once upon a time, a brave...") and let their imaginations take the reins.

- **Twist the Tale:**

Challenge them to rewrite classic stories with a positive twist. Imagine Cinderella standing up for herself, or Goldilocks befriending the bears. This empowers them to rewrite their own stories and overcome challenges.

- **Mirror, Mirror on the Wall:**

Encourage them to act out stories, express emotions through characters, and explore different perspectives. Imagine them stepping onto the stage of their own lives, conducting their own symphony of resilience and optimism.

The Playful Powerhouse:

- **Fortress of Fun:**

Ditch structured activities and embrace open-ended play. Provide blankets, pillows, and chairs, and let them build a fort – their imagination will do the rest! Encourage them to act out stories, create characters, and embark on epic adventures within their very own fortress.

- **"Yes, And…" Games:**

Introduce the simple rule of "Yes, and…" where each participant builds upon the previous person's idea. This fosters collaboration, creative thinking, and problem-solving skills in a fun and imaginative way.

- **Nature's Playground:**

Go beyond the backyard! Explore parks, forests, or beaches, where nature ignites curiosity, encourages movement, and reduces stress. Let them create stories inspired by the natural world, building a connection with their environment and fostering positive thinking.

Remember, imagination is a muscle that thrives on exercise. By weaving these engaging storytelling and play activities into their lives, you're not just giving them temporary entertainment, you're equipping them with the power to shape their own narratives, cultivate optimistic thinking, and conduct their own beautiful symphony of imagination and resilience.

Stay tuned for more actionable hacks and science-backed strategies to further optimize your child's imagination toolkit. Together, let's raise a generation of creative thinkers, problem-solvers, and dreamers, ready to write their own happy endings!

Igniting Imagination
Playful Hacks for Happiness & Optimism

Forget rigid routines and structured activities, we're about to biohack happiness through the power of play! Think of your child as a conductor, but instead of an orchestra, they're leading a grand symphony of imagination, resilience, and positive emotions. Buckle up, parents, educators, and play champions, because it's time to turn playtime into a potent tool for fostering optimism and emotional well-being!

Ditch the adult agenda, embrace the magic of make-believe. Play isn't just fun and games; it's a powerful learning lab for emotional intelligence. Through playful exploration, children experiment with different situations, navigate challenges, and build coping mechanisms - all while having a blast!

The Playful Powerhouse:

- **Open-Ended Explorations:**
Ditch rigid plans and embrace open-ended play. Provide simple materials like blocks, dress-up clothes, or art supplies,

and let their imaginations soar. This fosters creative problem-solving and the ability to adapt to new situations, building resilience.

- **Collaborative Creations:**

Encourage cooperative play with friends or siblings. Building forts, writing stories together, or putting on plays fosters communication, empathy, and conflict resolution skills – key ingredients for emotional well-being.

- **Nature's Playground:**

Get outdoors! Exploring parks, forests, or beaches ignites curiosity, encourages movement, and reduces stress. This connection with nature boosts mood, promotes relaxation, and fosters a sense of wonder, contributing to overall positive emotions.

Remember, play is more than just fun; it's a training ground for life. By providing opportunities for open-ended, collaborative, and nature-based play, you're not just giving them temporary entertainment, you're equipping them with the tools to navigate challenges, manage emotions, and cultivate a lasting sense of optimism. Their playful adventures become a symphony of emotional intelligence, preparing them to conduct their own beautiful melody of well-being throughout life.

Stay tuned for more actionable hacks and science-backed strategies to further optimize your child's play toolkit. Together, let's raise a generation of resilient, optimistic individuals who thrive through the power of playful exploration!

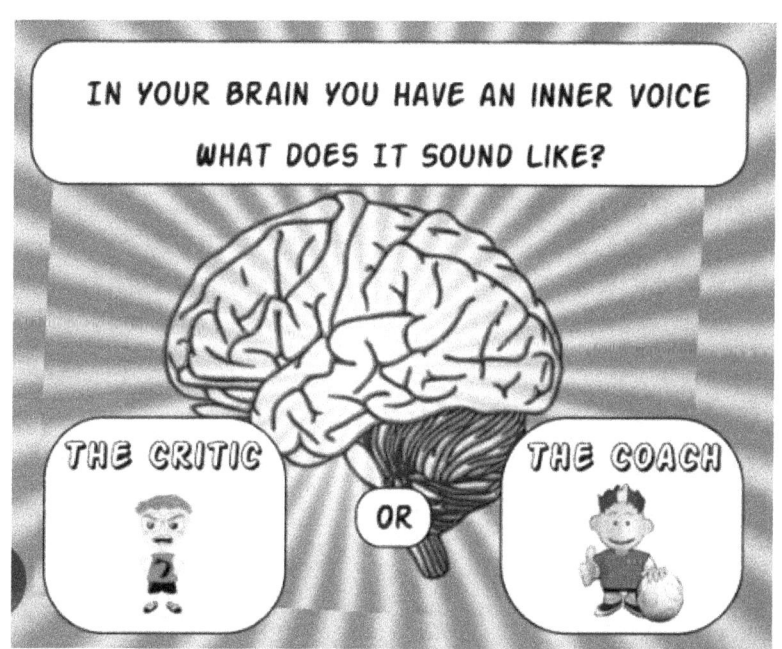

LESSON 7

TAMING THE INNER CRITIC

Biohacking Positive Self-Talk Like a Boss

Remember the symphony orchestra metaphor? We've tuned the instruments – positive mindset, resilience, communication, empathy, and connection – but wait, there's an unwelcome guest in the stands: the inner critic. Don't worry, though! We're not just silencing it, we're biohacking positive self-talk like a boss and helping children transform that critic into a supportive coach. Buckle up, parents, educators, and inner critic wranglers, it's time to conduct a symphony of self-acceptance and empower children to manage negative thoughts!

Forget fear-mongering, focus on understanding. We're not trying to demonize the inner critic, just identify its patterns and help children develop coping mechanisms. Think of it as understanding a tricky instrument in the orchestra – once you know its quirks, you can adjust them to create beautiful harmony.

The Inner Critic Coach:

- **Thought Detectives:** Help children identify negative thought patterns. Train them to catch self-critical phrases like "I'm not good enough" or "I'll never succeed." Think of it as spotting dissonant notes in the music and understanding their source.

- **Challenge the Critic:** Encourage them to question negative thoughts. Ask them if the critic is being overly harsh, if the thought is based on facts, or if they'd say the same thing to a friend. Imagine a debate between the conductor and the critic, where reason prevails over negativity.

- **Reframe the Melody:** Teach them to reframe negative thoughts into positive affirmations. Instead of "I'm failing," turn it into "I'm learning and growing." Think of it as adjusting the notes to create a more uplifting and empowering melody.

Remember, taming the inner critic is a continuous process. By equipping children with these tools for identifying and transforming negative thoughts, you're not just giving them temporary relief, you're teaching them self-compassion, building resilience, and conducting their own symphony of self-belief and positive self-talk.

Stay tuned for more actionable hacks and science-backed strategies to further optimize your child's inner critic toolkit. Together, let's raise a generation of confident, self-aware individuals who silence their inner critics and conduct their own beautiful symphonies of self-acceptance and success!

Taming the Inner Critic
Ninja Hacks for Positive Self-Talk

Forget silencing your child's inner critic – we're going full Jedi Mind Trick! Let's biohack their self-talk into a force for good with ninja-level reframing strategies. Imagine their mind as a powerful orchestra, but with a discordant critic sabotaging the harmony. Buckle up, parents, educators, and inner critic wranglers, it's time to conduct a symphony of self-acceptance and empower children to transform negativity into empowering affirmations!

Ditch the negativity detox, embrace the reframing revolution. We're not just removing negative thoughts, we're transforming them into fuel for positive growth. Think of it like turning weeds into beautiful flowers, enriching the mental garden for a vibrant symphony of self-belief.

The Reframing Revolution:

- **Fact-Check the Critic:**

Help children challenge negative thoughts with reason. Ask them if the critic's claims are true, based on evidence, or just grumpy speculation. Imagine them wielding a light-Saber of logic, deflecting negativity with facts and reason.

- **Perspective Power-Up:**

Encourage them to see things from different angles. Ask them how a friend might view the situation, or what their future selves would say. Think of it as expanding the orchestra's instruments, adding diverse perspectives to create a richer soundscape.

- **Humour Hack:**

Laughter is the best medicine! Teach them to use humor to defuse negativity. Help them create silly voices for their inner critic, turn self-doubt into jokes, or find the absurdity in negative thoughts. Imagine disarming the critic with laughter, like a well-timed cymbal crash adding unexpected joy to the melody.

- Affirmation Arsenal: Equip them with a toolkit of positive affirmations. Help them craft personalized statements like "I am capable," "I am worthy," and "I can learn from mistakes." Think of these as powerful mantras, each note reinforcing self-belief and resilience.

Remember, reframing is a skill that takes practice. By providing these ninja-level strategies and encouraging consistent reframing, you're not just giving them temporary relief, you're teaching them self-compassion, building mental strength, and conducting their own beautiful symphony of positive self-talk, silencing the inner critic permanently!

Stay tuned for more actionable hacks and science-backed strategies to further optimize your child's inner critic toolkit.

Together, let's raise a generation of confident, self-aware individuals who wield the power of reframing, conducting their own beautiful symphonies of self-acceptance and success!

Taming the Inner Critic
Cultivating Compassion & Conducting Self-Acceptance

Remember the symphony orchestra metaphor? We've tuned the instruments – positive mindset, resilience, communication, empathy, and connection – but there's still a discordant note: the inner critic. Don't fret! We're not just silencing it, we're biohacking self-compassion and conducting a beautiful melody of self-acceptance. Buckle up, parents, educators, and inner critic wranglers, because it's time to empower children to manage negative thoughts with kindness and understanding!

Ditch the self-blame spiral, focus on self-love's crescendo. We're not about guilt trips or punishment; we're about building a foundation of self-compassion that helps children navigate challenges with kindness and acceptance. Think of it as adding a warm, supportive cello to the orchestra, enriching the melody with empathy and understanding.

The Self-Compassion Symphony:

- **Kindness Conductor:**

Help children befriend their inner critic. Instead of viewing it as an enemy, encourage them to see it as a worried friend who needs guidance. Imagine them conducting a conversation with their critic, offering reassurance and understanding.

- **Thoughtful Timeouts:**

Teach them to pause during negative self-talk. Encourage them to take a deep breath, step back, and observe their thoughts without judgment. Think of it as a temporary rest for the critic, allowing for a moment of calm reflection.

- **"Mistakes Make Us Magnificent" Mantra:**

Reframe mistakes as learning opportunities. Help them see challenges as stepping stones to growth, not failures. Encourage them to say, "I made a mistake, but I can learn from it and try again," like a triumphant trumpet section overcoming a missed note.

- **Self-Care Serenade:**

Prioritize activities that promote self-compassion. Encourage hobbies, relaxation techniques, or spending time in nature. Imagine these as calming strings sections, harmonizing with the rest of the orchestra to create a peaceful soundscape.

Remember, self-compassion is a lifelong journey. By providing these tools and fostering a culture of understanding, you're not just giving them temporary relief, you're teaching them valuable life lessons about self-acceptance, building emotional resilience, and conducting their own beautiful symphony of self-love, silencing the inner critic with the powerful melody of compassion!

Stay tuned for more actionable hacks and science-backed strategies to further optimize your child's self-compassion toolkit. Together, let's raise a gener ation of confident, self-aware individuals who embrace their imperfections, conduct their own beautiful symphonies of self-acceptance, and silence their inner critics with the power of self-love!

LESSON 8

CELEBRATING EFFORT

Ditching Perfection, Embracing Progress Like a Boss

Forget the finish line mentality and its crushing perfectionism! We're all about biohacking happiness by celebrating effort and progress, not the elusive prize of being flawless. Imagine your child's confidence as a thriving garden – perfectionism is a weed, effort and progress are the sunshine and water. Buckle up, parents, educators, and growth champions, because it's time to conduct a symphony of self-worth, where every step forward is celebrated!

Ditch the gold medal myth, focus on the joyful journey. We're not chasing some unattainable ideal, we're appreciating every step of the learning process. Think of it like valuing each note in a musician's practice, not just the final concert performance.

The Progress Powerhouse:

- **Effort Excavation:**

Help children identify and appreciate their effort. Point out their hard work, persistence, and strategies, not just the outcome. Remember, the effort is often hidden – unearth it and shower them with genuine praise!

- **Failure Fiesta:**

Reframe mistakes as opportunities to learn and grow. Instead of dwelling on what went wrong, throw a "learning party" to celebrate the lessons learned. Think of it as a chance to experiment with different notes, leading to a richer, more nuanced melody.

- **"Growth Mindset Groove":** Encourage them to adopt a growth mindset. Instead of "I can't do this," guide them to say, "This is tough, but I can learn from it and get better." Think of it as shifting the tempo, turning challenges into exciting opportunities for improvement.

Remember, perfectionism is a joy thief. By celebrating effort and progress, you're not just giving them temporary praise, you're building a foundation of self-worth, boosting resilience, and conducting their own beautiful symphony of intrinsic motivation, where every note represents the joy of learning and growing!

Celebrate even small achievements, appreciate each step taken, each effort put-in towards the goal

Stay tuned for more actionable hacks and science-backed strategies to further optimize your child's progress celebration toolkit. Together, let's raise a generation of confident, resilient individuals who ditch the perfectionism trap, embrace the learning journey, and conduct their own beautiful symphonies of self-worth and achievement!

Celebrating Effort

Biohacking Happiness with Progress Parties, Not Perfection Paralysis

Remember the tyranny of the finish line, where achievement overshadows the journey? We're ditching that noise! Buckle up, parents, educators, and growth champions, because it's time to conduct a symphony of self-worth where effort and learning become the rockstars, not some unattainable gold medal. Think of it as biohacking happiness by shifting the focus from the distant applause to the joy of each practiced note.

Ditch the "perfect report card" pressure, focus on the "learning adventure" prize. We're not about comparing scores or chasing external validation; we're about celebrating the intrinsic rewards of growth and personal improvement. Imagine each conquered challenge as a new instrument mastered, adding depth and richness to their own unique orchestra of knowledge and skill.

The Progress Powerhouse:

- **Effort Excavation:**

Become an effort archaeologist, unearthing and celebrating the hidden gems of hard work. Don't just praise the A on the test, but highlight the late nights studying, the persistence through frustration, and the clever strategies they employed. Every drop of sweat deserves a spotlight!

- **Failure Fiesta:**

Rebrand mistakes as stepping stones to mastery. Instead of dwelling on the misstep, throw a "learning party" to celebrate the valuable lessons gained. Think of it as experimenting with different notes, each one shaping their musicality and preparing them for a more powerful performance.

- **"Growth Mindset Groove":**

Help them ditch the "fixed mindset" blues and embrace the growth mindset groove. Instead of "I can't do this," guide them to jam with the mantra, "This is tough, but I can learn and get better." It's all about shifting the tempo, turning challenges into exciting opportunities for improvisation and personal evolution.

Remember, perfectionism is a joy-sucking vampire. By focusing on effort and progress, you're not just offering temporary praise; you're building a fortress of self-worth, resilience, and intrinsic motivation. Their self-belief becomes the conductor, leading them to compose their own beautiful symphony of learning and personal growth, where every note resonates with the power of "I did it!" and "I can do it!"

Stay tuned for more actionable hacks and science-backed strategies to further optimize your child's progress celebration toolkit. Together, let's raise a generation of confident, resilient individuals who ditch the perfectionism trap, embrace the learning journey, and conduct their own beautiful symphonies of self-worth and achievement!

Celebrating Effort

Small Wins, Big Gains - Ditching Perfection, Embracing Progress Like a Boss

Forget the finish line mirage and its crushing perfectionism! We're about biohacking happiness by celebrating small wins and fueling perseverance, not the elusive prize of being flawless. Imagine your child's motivation as a thriving garden – perfectionism is a weed, small wins and progress are the sunshine and water. Buckle up, parents, educators, and growth champions, because it's time to conduct a symphony of self-worth, where every step forward is a joyful celebration!

Ditch the gold medal myth, focus on the daily victory dance. We're not chasing some unattainable ideal; we're appreciating every conquered challenge, every mastered skill, every "I figured it out!" moment. Think of it like cheering for each note in a musician's practice, not just the final concert performance.

The Progress Powerhouse:

- **Effort Excavation:**

Become a small win detective, uncovering and celebrating the hidden gems of hard work. Don't just praise the final project, but highlight the daily effort, the persistence through setbacks, and the creative problem-solving they employed. Every hurdle jumped deserves a high-five!

- **Failure Fiesta:**

Reframe mistakes as stepping stones to success. Instead of dwelling on the misstep, throw a "learning party" to celebrate the valuable lessons learned and the resilience displayed. Think of it as experimenting with different notes, each one shaping their musicality and preparing them for a more powerful performance.

- **"Growth Mindset Groove":**

Help them ditch the "fixed mindset" blues and embrace the growth mindset groove. Instead of "I can't do this," guide them to jam with the mantra, "This is tough, but I can learn and get better." It's all about shifting the tempo, turning challenges into exciting opportunities for improvement and personal evolution.

Remember, perfectionism is a progress-killing villain. By celebrating small wins and encouraging perseverance, you're not just giving them temporary praise; you're building a foundation of self-worth, resilience, and intrinsic motivation. Their self-belief becomes the conductor, leading them to compose their own beautiful symphony of learning and personal growth, where every note resonates with the power of "I did it!" and "I can do it!"

Stay tuned for more actionable hacks and science-backed strategies to further optimize your child's progress celebration toolkit. Together, let's raise a generation of confident, resilient individuals who ditch the perfectionism trap, embrace the learning journey, and conduct their own beautiful symphonies of self-worth and achievement!

LESSON 9

NAVIGATING THE DIGITAL WORLD

Biohacking Positivity in the Age of Likes & Algorithms

Remember the symphony orchestra metaphor? We've tuned the instruments – positive mindset, resilience, communication, empathy, and connection – but wait, there's a new section added: the digital world. Don't worry, though! We're not silencing it, but biohacking it for positivity in a world of likes, algorithms, and constant connectivity. Buckle up, parents, educators, and digital champions, because it's time to conduct a symphony of well-being where technology enhances, not disrupts, our children's mental health!

Ditch the digital detox myth, focus on mindful integration. We're not demonizing technology; we're about understanding its impact and empowering children to navigate it consciously. Think of it like learning a new instrument in the orchestra – mastering its capabilities while maintaining harmonious balance with the other sections.

The Digital Wellness Maestro:

- **Screen Time Samurai:**

Become a screen time detective, identifying healthy usage patterns and setting clear boundaries. Don't just limit screen time, but replace it with enriching activities, fostering a holistic approach to digital wellness.

- **Content Curator:**

Be a critical thinking coach, helping children evaluate online content. Encourage them to question misinformation, identify biases, and seek diverse perspectives. Think of it like teaching them to discern between beautiful melodies and discordant noise.

- **Connection Conductor:**

Prioritize real-world connection over virtual interactions. Encourage face-to-face communication, outdoor activities, and social engagement. Remember, the orchestra thrives on the interplay of its members, not just individual instruments.

- **Mindful Moments:**

Promote digital mindfulness practices. Encourage them to be present in the moment while using technology, taking breaks, and avoiding multitasking. Imagine them conducting moments of calm amidst the digital symphony, reducing stress and boosting mental well-being.

Remember, digital well-being is a continuous practice. By providing these mindful strategies and fostering open communication, you're not just giving them temporary relief, you're equipping them with the tools to navigate the digital world with awareness, resilience, and a positive mindset. Their digital experience becomes a harmonious instrument in their lives, enriching their overall symphony of well-being and growth.

Stay tuned for more actionable hacks and science-backed strategies to further optimize your child's digital wellness toolkit. Together, let's raise a generation of digitally savvy, mindful individuals who conduct their own beautiful symphonies of well-being, using technology as a tool for connection, creativity, and positive growth!

Navigating the Digital World
From Screen Zombies to Tech Titans
Crafting Healthy Boundaries & Owning Your Digital Experience

Remember the symphony orchestra metaphor? We've tuned the instruments – positive mindset, resilience, communication, empathy, and connection – but wait, there's a new section added: the digital world. Don't worry, though! We're not silencing it, but biohacking it for positivity in a world of likes, algorithms, and constant connectivity. Buckle up, parents, educators, and digital champions, because it's time to conduct a symphony of well-being where technology enhances, not disrupts, our children's mental health!

Ditch the digital detox myth, focus on mindful integration with boundaries like a boss. We're not demonizing technology; we're about understanding its impact and empowering children to navigate it responsibly. Think of it like setting smart rules for each instrument in the orchestra – maximizing their potential while maintaining harmonious balance with the rest.

The Digital Boundary Dojo:

- **Screen Time Samurai:**

Become a screen time detective, identifying healthy usage patterns and setting clear, consistent boundaries. Don't just limit screen time, but create screen-free zones and time slots, fostering a holistic approach to digital wellness. Think of it like establishing rest periods for each instrument, ensuring optimal performance and preventing burnout.

- **App Audit:**

Be a mindful guardian, helping children curate their digital environment. Guide them to choose enriching apps and games, avoiding excessive or age-inappropriate content. Imagine them selecting instruments that complement the overall melody, creating a rich and fulfilling soundscape.

- **Master of Mindfulness:**

Promote digital mindfulness practices. Encourage them to be present in the moment while using technology, taking regular breaks, and avoiding multitasking. Think of it like conducting moments of quiet reflection amidst the digital symphony, reducing stress and boosting mental focus.

- **Open Communication Conductor:**

Foster open and honest communication about online experiences. Encourage them to share their concerns and challenges without judgment, creating a safe space for discussion and guidance. Remember, the conductor ensures harmony by understanding each instrument's needs – open communication is key.

Remember, digital well-being is a continuous practice. By providing these actionable strategies and fostering open communication, you're not just giving them temporary relief, you're equipping them with the tools to navigate the digital world with awareness, resilience, and a positive mindset. Their digital experience becomes a harmonious instrument in their lives, enriching their overall symphony of well-being and growth.

Stay tuned for more actionable hacks and science-backed strategies to further optimize your child's digital wellness toolkit. Together, let's raise a generation of digitally savvy, mindful individuals who conduct their own beautiful symphonies of well-being, using technology as a tool for connection, creativity, and positive growth!

Navigating the Digital World
From Keyboard Warriors to Digital Crusaders Promoting Positive Engagement & Owning Your Online Identity

Remember the symphony orchestra metaphor? We've tuned the instruments – positive mindset, resilience, communication, empathy, and connection – but wait, there's a new section added: the digital world. Don't worry, though! We're not silencing it, but biohacking it for positivity in a world of likes, algorithms, and constant connectivity. Buckle up, parents, educators, and digital champions, because it's time to conduct a symphony of well-being where technology enhances, not disrupts, our children's mental health!

Ditch the "digital detox" myth, focus on mindful integration and proactive citizenship. We're not demonizing technology; we're about empowering children to navigate it responsibly and contribute positively. Think of it like mastering each instrument in the orchestra, not just for individual performance, but for creating a powerful, harmonious collective sound.

The Digital Citizen Maestro:

- **Positivity Powerhouse:**

Encourage positive online interactions. Guide them to be respectful, kind, and inclusive in their digital communication. Imagine them crafting melodies of empathy and understanding, enriching the online experience for everyone.

- **Critical Thinking Conductor:**

Be a media literacy coach, helping children evaluate online information critically. Encourage them to question sources, identify biases, and fact-check information. Think of it like discerning between accurate notes and discordant noise, ensuring a well-informed and harmonious digital experience.

- **Cyberhero Academy:**

Foster digital responsibility. Teach them about online safety, privacy settings, and cyberbullying prevention. Imagine them wielding their digital skills like brave knights, protecting themselves and others in the online community.

- **Positive Content Creators:**

Promote creative and responsible content creation. Encourage them to express themselves positively online, share their talents, and contribute to constructive online communities. Think of it like composing their own unique melodies that inspire and uplift others, adding richness and variety to the digital symphony.

Remember, digital citizenship is a continuous learning journey. By providing these actionable strategies and fostering open communication, you're not just giving them temporary relief, you're equipping them with the tools to navigate the digital world with awareness, responsibility, and a positive mindset. Their digital experience becomes a harmonious instrument in their lives, enriching their overall symphony of well-being and growth, and contributing to a more positive and constructive online world for everyone.

Stay tuned for more actionable hacks and science-backed strategies to further optimize your child's digital citizenship toolkit. Together, let's raise a generation of digitally responsible, mindful individuals who conduct their own beautiful symphonies of well-being, using technology as a tool for connection, creativity, positive impact, and ethical citizenship!

LESSON 10

GROWING TOGETHER

Biohacking a Family Growth Mindset Like a Boss

Forget the fixed mindset blues and its "we can't learn, grow, or evolve" narrative! We're all about biohacking a positive growth mindset for your entire family or community. Think of it like conducting a symphony of continuous learning and self-improvement, where every member contributes their unique talents and growth potential. Buckle up, parents, educators, and lifelong learning champions, because it's time to create a harmonious environment where everyone thrives!

Ditch the "fixed family" label, focus on the "growth groove." We're not about rigid roles or limitations; we're about empowering everyone to learn, challenge themselves, and celebrate progress. Think of it like every member adding their own instrument to the orchestra, creating a richer, more dynamic soundscape.

The Family Growth Groove:

- **Effort Excavation:**

Become growth mindset detectives, uncovering and celebrating hidden gems of effort in each other. Don't just praise the A on the test, but highlight the perseverance through challenges, the creative problem-solving, and the willingness to try new things. Every hurdle jumped deserves a cheer!

- **Failure Fiesta:**

Rebrand mistakes as stepping stones to mastery. Instead of dwelling on setbacks, throw a "learning party" to celebrate the valuable lessons learned and the resilience displayed. Imagine it like experimenting with different notes, each one shaping the family's musicality and preparing them for a more powerful performance.

- **"Growth Mindset Groove":**

Help everyone ditch the "fixed mindset" blues and embrace the growth mindset groove. Encourage each other with mantras like, "This is tough, but we can learn and get better together." It's all about shifting the tempo, turning challenges into exciting opportunities for collective growth and positive change.

- **Lifelong Learning Lab:**

Foster a culture of continuous learning. Explore new interests together, take on challenges as a team, and embrace diverse learning styles. Think of it like expanding the orchestra's repertoire, adding exciting new instruments and exploring different genres to keep the melody fresh and engaging.

Remember, a growth mindset is a family affair. By providing these actionable hacks and fostering a supportive, encouraging environment, you're not just creating temporary positivity, you're building a foundation for lifelong learning, resilience, and personal growth for everyone. Your family or community becomes a symphony of empowered individuals, each contributing their unique talents and growth potential to create a beautiful and ever-evolving masterpiece of shared learning and positive change.

Stay tuned for more actionable hacks and science-backed strategies to further optimize your family's or community's growth mindset toolkit. Together, let's create a world where lifelong learning, collaboration, and personal growth are the norm, and everyone has the opportunity to conduct their own beautiful symphony of self-improvement!

Growing Together

Biohacking Family Wellbeing Like a Boss - Self-Care & Role Model Rockstar Status

Forget the burnout blues and the "we're too busy to learn" narrative! We're all about biohacking family well-being to fuel your lifelong learning journey. Think of it like conducting a symphony of self-care, growth, and connection, where everyone thrives by prioritizing their individual needs and inspiring one another to reach their full potential. Buckle up, parents, educators, and growth champions, because it's time to create a harmonious environment where self-care and learning go hand-in-hand!

Ditch the "martyr parent" badge, focus on the "wellbeing warrior" shield. We're not about sacrificing ourselves on the altar of achievement; we're about prioritizing self-care as the foundation for individual and collective growth. Think of it like tuning each instrument in the orchestra before a performance – ensuring everyone is in peak condition to contribute their best music.

The Wellbeing Symphony:

- **Self-Care Serenade**:

Encourage individualized self-care practices for each member. Whether it's meditation, exercise, creative hobbies, or spending time in nature, help everyone discover what fuels their energy and well-being. Imagine them playing their instruments with renewed vigor and joy, enriching the overall melody.

- **Positivity Power-Up:**

Be a positive role model. Show your own commitment to learning, embrace challenges with enthusiasm, and celebrate everyone's efforts. Imagine radiating contagious optimism, like a conductor infusing the orchestra with their passion and belief.

- **Open Communication Chorus:**

Foster open and honest communication about individual needs and feelings. Create a safe space where everyone can express themselves authentically, ask for support, and celebrate each other's successes. Think of it like harmonious communication between orchestra sections, ensuring everyone feels heard and valued.

- **Compassionate Conductor:**

Lead with empathy and understanding. Acknowledge individual challenges, offer support without judgment, and celebrate diversity in learning styles and preferences. Imagine wielding your leadership like a compassionate conductor, guiding everyone towards personal growth and fulfilment.

Remember, self-care and positive role modeling are essential melodies in the symphony of family wellbeing. By providing these actionable hacks and fostering a supportive, encouraging environment, you're not just creating temporary positivity, you're building a foundation for lifelong learning, resilience, and personal growth for everyone. Your family becomes a symphony of empowered individuals, each contributing their unique talents and growth potential to create a beautiful and ever-evolving masterpiece of shared learning and positive change.

Stay tuned for more actionable hacks and science-backed strategies to further optimize your family's or community's growth mindset toolkit. Together, let's create a world where lifelong learning, collaboration, and personal growth are the norm, and everyone has the opportunity to conduct their own beautiful symphony of self-improvement!

Growing Together
Biohacking a Family Growth Groove Like a Boss

Forget the fixed mindset blues and its "we can't learn, grow, or evolve" narrative! We're all about biohacking a positive growth mindset for your entire family or community. Think of it like conducting a symphony of continuous learning and self-improvement, where every member contributes their unique talents and growth potential. Buckle up, parents, educators, and lifelong learning champions, because it's time to create a harmonious environment where everyone thrives!

Ditch the "fixed family" label, focus on the "growth groove." We're not about rigid roles or limitations; we're about empowering everyone to learn, challenge themselves, and celebrate progress. Think of it like every member adding their own instrument to the orchestra, creating a richer, more dynamic soundscape.

The Family Growth Groove:

- **Challenge Crasher Crew:**

Transform challenges into exciting opportunities for growth. Instead of shying away from difficulties, view them as stepping stones to mastery. Encourage everyone to say,

"Bring it on!" with the same enthusiasm as a rockstar hitting the stage.

- **Failure Fiesta:**

Rebrand mistakes as valuable learning experiences. Ditch the shame and throw a "learning party" to celebrate the lessons learned and the resilience displayed. Think of it like experimenting with different notes, each one refining the family's musicality and preparing them for a more powerful performance.

- **"Growth Mindset Groove":**

Help everyone ditch the "fixed mindset" blues and embrace the growth mindset groove. Encourage each other with mantras like, "This is tough, but we can learn and get better together." It's all about shifting the tempo, turning challenges into exciting opportunities for collective growth and positive change.

- **Lifelong Learning Lab:**

Foster a culture of continuous curiosity. Embrace new experiences, explore diverse learning styles, and encourage everyone to ask questions and seek answers. Think of it like expanding the orchestra's repertoire, adding exciting new instruments and exploring different genres to keep the melody fresh and engaging.

Remember, a growth mindset is a family affair. By providing these actionable hacks and fostering a supportive, encouraging environment, you're not just creating temporary positivity, you're building a foundation for lifelong learning, resilience, and personal growth for everyone. Your family or community becomes a symphony of empowered individuals, each contributing their unique talents and growth potential to create a beautiful and ever-evolving masterpiece of shared learning and positive change.

Stay tuned for more actionable hacks and science-backed strategies to further optimize your family's or community's growth mindset toolkit. Together, let's create a world where lifelong learning, collaboration, and personal growth are the norm, and everyone has the opportunity to conduct their own beautiful symphony of self-improvement!

CONCLUSION

We can conclude that cultivating a positive mindset is crucial for achieving happiness and success in life. Positive thinking improves mental and physical health, increases self-esteem and confidence, improves relationships, and enhances problem-solving skills…

Although Parenting is a Roller-Coaster ride, and no one can provide the fixed strategy for it because every Kid is different and special in their own way. Think, analyse and then decide what best works for your **CHAMP**!!! I provided only few concepts that can be used to get out the "**Best Version of Your Kid**"…

Looking forward to share more experiences with you all in the near future…

Stay tuned with for more Happy Books coming soon!!!!

ACKNOWLEDGEMENTS

My deepest gratitude to all the individuals in past and present who shared the knowledge on the Law of Attraction, Manifestation techniques, tips and tricks on creating Positive Mindset.

My deepest thanks to my main Support system in life that is "My Family". Special thanks to my Husband, he is moreover an friend for life, who never judged or doubted my capability and encouraged me in all my endeavors may it be job opportunities, trainings or book writing.

My Special thanks to my Parents and In-Laws because of whom I could leave back the worry of household chores and concentrate over my growth. Elders have been always the source of Motivation for me throughout the life.

My love and thanks to my Kiddos Sanvi and Shourya, who are my greatest teachers. They say " Experience is the best Teacher ". And these little ones give me that experience and make me a better Parent each day which inspired me the most to write this book.

Acknowledgements

From the bottom of my heart, Thank each and everyone who helped me directly or indirectly. Special thanks to all "My Readers".

www.ingramcontent.com/pod-product-compliance
Lightning Source LLC
LaVergne TN
LVHW061556070526
838199LV00077B/7065